Poems 1950–1966
A Selection

by Thom Gunn

★

THE SENSE OF MOVEMENT
MY SAD CAPTAINS
TOUCH
FIGHTING TERMS
SELECTED POEMS
(with Ted Hughes)

POEMS 1950-1966

A Selection

by

THOM GUNN

FABER AND FABER
24 Russell Square
London

First published in this edition in 1969
by Faber and Faber Limited
24 Russell Square London WC1
Printed in Great Britain by
R. MacLehose & Co Ltd
The University Press Glasgow
All rights reserved

SBN 571 08845 7

© Thom Gunn 1954, 1957, 1961, 1966, 1967
© this selection by Thom Gunn
1969

Contents

The Wound

The huge wound in my head began to heal
About the beginning of the seventh week.
Its valleys darkened, its villages became still:
For joy I did not move and dared not speak;
Not doctors would cure it, but time, its patient skill.

And constantly my mind returned to Troy.
After I sailed the seas I fought in turn
On both sides, sharing even Helen's joy
Of place, and growing up — to see Troy burn —
As Neoptolemus, that stubborn boy.

I lay and rested as prescription said.
Manoeuvred with the Greeks, or sallied out
Each day with Hector. Finally my bed
Became Achilles' tent, to which the lout
Thersites came reporting numbers dead.

I was myself: subject to no man's breath:
My own commander was my enemy.
And while my belt hung up, sword in the sheath,
Thersites shambled in and breathlessly
Cackled about my friend Patroclus' death.

I called for armour, rose, and did not reel.
But, when I thought, rage at his noble pain
Flew to my head, and turning I could feel
My wound break open wide. Over again
I had to let those storm-lit valleys heal.

Here Come the Saints

Here come the saints: so near, so innocent,
They gravely cross the field of moonlit snow;
We villagers gape humbly at the show.
No act or gesture can suggest intent.
They only wait until the first cock crow
Batters our ears, and with abrupt and violent
Motions into the terrible dark wood they go.

To His Cynical Mistress

And love is then no more than a compromise?
An impermanent treaty waiting to be signed
   By the two enemies?
While the calculating Cupid feigning impartial-blind
Drafts it, promising peace, both leaders wise
To his antics sign but secretly double their spies.

On each side is the ignorant animal nation,
Jostling friendly in streets, enjoying in good faith
   This celebration,
Forgetting their enmity with cheers and drunken breath;
But for them there has not been yet amalgamation:
The leaders calmly plot assassination.

Lazarus Not Raised

He was not changed. His friends around the grave
Stared down upon his greasy placid face
Bobbing on shadows; nothing it seemed could save
His body now from the sand below their wave,
The scheduled miracle not taking place.

He lay inert beneath those outstretched hands
Which beckoned him to life. Though coffin-case
Was ready to hold life and winding-bands
At his first stir would loose the frozen glands,
The scheduled miracle did not take place.

O Lazarus, distended body laid
Glittering without weight on death's surface:
Rise now before you sink, we dare not wade
Into that sad marsh where (the mourners cried)
The scheduled miracle cannot take place.

When first aroused and given thoughts and breath,
He chose to amble at his normal pace
In childhood fields imaginary and safe —
Much like the trivial territory of death
(The miracle had not yet taken place);

He chose to spend his thoughts like this at first
And disregard the nag of offered grace,
Then chose to spend the rest of them in rest.
The final effort came, forward we pressed
To see the scheduled miracle take place:

Abruptly the corpse blinked and shook his head
Then sank again, sliding without a trace
From sight, to take slime on the deepest bed
Of vacancy. He had chosen to stay dead,
The scheduled miracle did not take place.

Nothing else changed. I saw somebody peer
Stooping, into the oblong box of space.
His friends had done their best: without such fear
Without that terrified awakening glare,
The scheduled miracle would have taken place.

A Mirror for Poets

It was a violent time. Wheels, racks, and fires
In every writer's mouth, and not mere rant.
Certain shrewd herdsmen, between twisted wires
Of penalty folding the realm, were thanked
For organizing spies and secret police
By richness in the flock, which they could fleece.

Hacks in the Fleet and nobles in the Tower:
Shakespeare must keep the peace, and Jonson's thumb
Be branded (for manslaughter), to the power
Of irons the admired Southampton's power was come.
Above all swayed the diseased and doubtful queen:
Her state canopied by the glamour of pain.

In this society the boundaries met
Of life and life, at danger; with no space
Being left between, except where might be set
That mathematical point whose time and place
Could not exist. Yet at this point they found
Arcadia, a fruitful permanent land.

The faint and stumbling crowds were dim to sight
Who had no time for pity or for terror:
Here moved the Forms, flooding like moonlight,
In which the act or thought perceived its error.
The hustling details, calmed and relevant.
Here mankind might behold its whole extent.

Here in a cave the Paphlagonian King
Crouched, waiting for his greater counterpart
Who one remove from likelihood may seem,
But several nearer to the human heart.
In exile from dimension, change by storm,
Here his huge magnanimity was born.

Yet the historians tell us, life meant less.
It was a violent time, and evil-smelling.
Jonson howled 'Hell's a grammar-school to this,'
But found renunciation well worth telling.
Winnowing with his flail of comedy
He showed coherence in society.

In street, in tavern, happening would cry
'I am myself, but part of something greater,
Find poets what that is, do not pass by,
For feel my fingers in your pia mater.
I am a cruelly insistent friend :
You cannot smile at me and make an end.'

The Beach Head

Now that a letter gives me ground at last
For starting from, I see my enterprise
Is more than application by a blast
Upon a trumpet slung beside a gate,
Security a fraud, and how unwise
Was disembarking on your Welfare State.

What should they see in you but what I see,
These friends you mention whom I do not know?
— You unsuspecting that a refugee
Might want the land complete, write in a tone
Too matter-of-fact, of small affairs below
Some minister's seduction of the Crown.

And even if they could be innocent,
They still applaud you, keep you satisfied
And occupy your time, which I resent.
Their werewolf lust and cunning are afraid
Of night-exposure in the hair, so hide
Distant as possible from my palisade.

I have my ground. A brain-sick enemy
Pacing the beach head he so plotted for
Which now seems trivial to his jealousy
And ignorance of the great important part,
I almost wish I had no narrow shore.
I seek a pathway to the country's heart.

Shall I be John a Gaunt and with my band
Of mad bloods pass in one spectacular dash,
Fighting before and after, through your land,
To issue out unharmed the farther side,
With little object other than panache
And showing what great odds may be defied?

That way achievement would at once be history:
Living inside, I would not know, the danger:
Hurry is blind and so does not brave mystery;
I should be led to underrate, by haste,
Your natural beauties: while I, hare-brained stranger,
Would not be much distinguished from the rest.

Or shall I wait and calculate my chances,
Consolidating this my inch-square base,
Picking off rival spies that tread your glances:
Then plan when you have least supplies or clothing
A pincer-move to end in an embrace,
And risk that your mild liking turn to loathing?

A Kind of Ethics

Old trees are witnesses:
    Their simple religion is forced into the cold,
    No intermediary gives them rules of conduct:
    All day without a minister they hold
Primitive services.

The power that they receive
    Out of the water, air and earth, can be
    Partial at best, for only on their branches
    Where leaves start from the black extremity
Can they be said to live.

The past that they have led
    Makes unapproachable and hidden sin:
    Deep in the foul confusion of their thicket,
    So dense no human being can go in,
Dry tangled twigs lie dead.

Among such broken wood
    Wild animals give birth to sharp toothed young:
    Unregenerate, they have no time for worship.
    Careless, out of a possibly bad may come
An undeniable good.

For a Birthday

I have reached a time when words no longer help:
Instead of guiding me across the moors
Strong landmarks in the uncertain out-of-doors,
Or like dependable friars on the Alp
Saving with wisdom and with brandy kegs,
They are gravel-stones, or tiny dogs which yelp
Biting my trousers, running round my legs.

Description and analysis degrade,
Limit, delay, slipped land from what has been;
And when we groan My Darling what we mean
Looked at more closely would too soon evade
The intellectual habit of our eyes;
And either the experience would fade
Or our approximations would be lies.

The snarling dogs are weight upon my haste,
Tons which I am detaching ounce by ounce.
All my agnostic irony I renounce
So I may climb to regions where I rest
In springs of speech, the dark before of truth:
The sweet moist wafer of your tongue I taste,
And find right meanings in your silent mouth.

Incident on a Journey

One night I reached a cave: I slept, my head
Full of the air. There came about daybreak
A red-coat soldier to the mouth, who said
'I am not living, in hell's pains I ache,
  But I regret nothing.'

His forehead had a bloody wound whose streaming
The pallid staring face illuminated.
Whether his words were mine or his, in dreaming
I found they were my deepest thoughts translated.
  '*I regret nothing:*

'Turn your closed eyes to see upon these walls
A mural scratched there by an earlier man,
And coloured with the blood of animals:
Showing humanity beyond its span,
  Regretting nothing.

'No plausible nostalgia, no brown shame
I had when treating with my enemies.
And always when a living impulse came
I acted, and my action made me wise.
  And I regretted nothing.

'I as possessor of unnatural strength
Was hunted, one day netted in a brawl;
A minute far beyond a minute's length
Took from me passion, strength, and life, and all.
    But I regretted nothing.

'Their triumph left my body in the dust;
The dust and beer still clotting in my hair
When I rise lonely, will-less. Where I must
I go, and what I must I bear.
    And I regret nothing.

'My lust runs yet and is unsatisfied,
My hate throbs yet but I am feeble-limbed;
If as an animal I could have died
My death had scattered instinct to the wind,
    Regrets as nothing.'

Later I woke. I started to my feet.
The valley light, the mist already going.
I was alive and felt my body sweet,
Uncaked blood in all its channels flowing.
    I would regret nothing.

On the Move

The blue jay scuffling in the bushes follows
Some hidden purpose, and the gust of birds
That spurts across the field, the wheeling swallows,
Have nested in the trees and undergrowth.
Seeking their instinct, or their poise, or both,
One moves with an uncertain violence
Under the dust thrown by a baffled sense
Or the dull thunder of approximate words.

On motorcycles, up the road, they come:
Small, black, as flies hanging in heat, the Boys,
Until the distance throws them forth, their hum
Bulges to thunder held by calf and thigh.
In goggles, donned impersonality,
In gleaming jackets trophied with the dust,
They strap in doubt — by hiding it, robust —
And almost hear a meaning in their noise.

Exact conclusion of their hardiness
Has no shape yet, but from known whereabouts
They ride, direction where the tires press.
They scare a flight of birds across the field:
Much that is natural, to the will must yield.
Men manufacture both machine and soul,
And use what they imperfectly control
To dare a future from the taken routes.

It is a part solution, after all.
One is not necessarily discord
On earth; or damned because, half animal,
One lacks direct instinct, because one wakes
Afloat on movement that divides and breaks.
One joins the movement in a valueless world,
Choosing it, till, both hurler and the hurled,
One moves as well, always toward, toward.

A minute holds them, who have come to go:
The self-defined, astride the created will
They burst away; the towns they travel through
Are home for neither bird nor holiness,
For birds and saints complete their purposes.
At worst, one is in motion; and at best,
Reaching no absolute, in which to rest,
One is always nearer by not keeping still.

Autumn Chapter in a Novel

Through woods, Mme Une Telle, a trifle ill
With idleness, but no less beautiful,
Walks with the young tutor, round their feet
Mob syllables slurred to a fine complaint,
Which in their time held off the natural heat.

The sun is distant, and they fill out space
Sweatless as watercolour under glass.
He kicks abruptly. But we may suppose
The leaves he scatters thus will settle back
In much the same position as they rose.

A tutor's indignation works on air,
Altering nothing; action bustles where,
Towards the pool by which they lately stood,
The husband comes discussing with his bailiff
Poachers, the broken fences round the wood.

Pighead! The poacher is at large, and lingers,
A dead mouse gripped between his sensitive fingers:
Fences already keep the live game out:
See how your property twists her parasol,
Hesitates in the tender trap of doubt.

Here they repair, here daily handle lightly
The brief excitements that disturb them nightly;
Sap draws back inch by inch, and to the ground
The words they uttered rustle constantly:
Silent, they watch the growing, weightless mound.

They leave at last a chosen element,
Resume the motions of their discontent;
She takes her sewing up, and he again
Names to her son the deserts on the globe,
And leaves thrust violently upon the pane.

The Silver Age

Do not enquire from the centurion nodding
At the corner, with his head gentle over
The swelling breastplate, where true Rome is found.
Even of Livy there are volumes lost.
All he can do is guide you through the moonlight.

When he moves, mark how his eager striding,
To which we know the darkness is a river
Sullen with mud, is easy as on ground.
We know it is a river never crossed
By any but some few who hate the moonlight.

And when he speaks, mark how his ancient wording
Is hard with indignation of a lover.
'I do not think our new Emperor likes the sound
Of turning squadrons or the last post.
Consorts with Christians, I think he lives in moonlight.'

Hurrying to show you his companions guarding,
He grips your arm like a cold strap of leather,
Then halts, earthpale, as he stares round and round.
What made this one fragment of a sunken coast
Remain, far out, to be beaten by the moonlight?

The Unsettled Motorcyclist's Vision of His Death

Across the open countryside,
Into the walls of rain I ride.
It beats my cheek, drenches my knees,
But I am being what I please.

The firm heath stops, and marsh begins.
Now we're at war : whichever wins
My human will cannot submit
To nature, though brought out of it.
The wheels sink deep ; the clear sound blurs :
Still, bent on the handle-bars,
I urge my chosen instrument
Against the mere embodiment.
The front wheel wedges fast between
Two shrubs of glazed insensate green
— Gigantic order in the rim
Of each flat leaf. Black eddies brim
Around my heel which, pressing deep,
Accelerates the waiting sleep.

I used to live in sound, and lacked
Knowledge of still or creeping fact,
But now the stagnant strips my breath,
Leant on my cheek in weight of death.
Though so oppressed I find I may
Through substance move. I pick my way,
Where death and life in one combine,
Through the dark earth that is not mine,
Crowded with fragments, blunt, unformed ;
While past my ear where noises swarmed
The marsh plant's white extremities,
Slow without patience, spread at ease
Invulnerable and soft, extend
With a quiet grasping toward their end.

And though the tubers, once I rot,
Reflesh my bones with pallid knot,
Till swelling out my clothes they feign
This dummy is a man again,
It is as servants they insist,
Without volition that they twist ;
And habit does not leave them tired,
By men laboriously acquired.

Cell after cell the plants convert
My special richness in the dirt:
All that they get, they get by chance.

And multiply in ignorance.

The Allegory of the Wolf Boy

The causes are in Time; only their issue
Is bodied in the flesh, the finite powers.
And how to guess he hides in that firm tissue
Seeds of division? At tennis and at tea
Upon the gentle lawn, he is not ours,
But plays us in a sad duplicity.

Tonight the boy, still boy open and blond,
Breaks from the house, wedges his clothes between
Two moulded garden urns, and goes beyond
His understanding, through the dark and dust:
Fields of sharp stubble, abandoned by machine
To the whirring enmity of insect lust.

As yet ungolden in the dense, hot night
The spikes enter his feet: he seeks the moon,
Which, with the touch of its infertile light,
Shall loose desires hoarded against his will
By the long urging of the afternoon.
Slowly the hard rim shifts above the hill.

White in the beam he stops, faces it square,
And the same instant leaping from the ground
Feels the familiar itch of close dark hair;
Then, clean exception to the natural laws,
Only to instinct and the moon being bound,
Drops on four feet. Yet he has bleeding paws.

Jesus and His Mother

My only son, more God's than mine,
Stay in this garden ripe with pears.
The yielding of their substance wears
A modest and contented shine:
And when they weep with age, not brine
But lazy syrup are their tears.
'I am my own and not my own.'

He seemed much like another man,
That silent foreigner who trod
Outside my door with lily rod:
How could I know what I began
Meeting the eyes more furious than
The eyes of Joseph, those of God?
I was my own and not my own.

And who are these twelve labouring men?
I do not understand your words:
I taught you speech, we named the birds,
You marked their big migrations then
Like any child. So turn again
To silence from the place of crowds.
'I am my own and not my own.'

Why are you sullen when I speak?
Here are your tools, the saw and knife
And hammer on your bench. Your life
Is measured here in week and week
Planed as the furniture you make,
And I will teach you like a wife
To be my own and all my own.

Who like an arrogant wind blown
Where he may please, needs no content?
Yet I remember how you went
To speak with scholars in furred gown.

I hear an outcry in the town;
Who carries that dark instrument?
'One all his own and not his own.'

Treading the green and nimble sward
I stare at a strange shadow thrown.
Are you the boy I bore alone,
No doctor near to cut the cord?
I cannot reach to call you Lord,
Answer me as my only son.
'I am my own and not my own.'

To Yvor Winters, 1955

I leave you in your garden.
                              In the yard
Behind it, run the airedales you have reared
With boxer's vigilance and poet's rigour:
Dog-generations you have trained the vigour
That few can breed to train and fewer still
Control with the deliberate human will.
And in the house there rest, piled shelf on shelf,
The accumulations that compose the self —
Poem and history: for if we use
Words to maintain the actions that we choose,
Our words, with slow defining influence,
Stay to mark out our chosen lineaments.

Continual temptation waits on each
To renounce his empire over thought and speech,
Till he submit his passive faculties
To evening, come where no resistance is;
The unmotivated sadness of the air
Filling the human with his own despair.
Where now lies power to hold the evening back?

Implicit in the grey is total black :
Denial of the discriminating brain
Brings the neurotic vision, and the vein
Of necromancy. All as relative
For mind as for the sense, we have to live
In a half-world, not ours nor history's,
And learn the false from half-true premisses.

But sitting in the dusk — though shapes combine,
Vague mass replacing edge and flickering line,
You keep both Rule and Energy in view,
Much power in each, most in the balanced two :
Ferocity existing in the fence
Built by an exercised intelligence.
Though night is always close, complete negation
Ready to drop on wisdom and emotion,
Night from the air or the carnivorous breath,
Still it is right to know the force of death,
And, as you do, persistent, tough in will,
Raise from the excellent the better still.

During an Absence

I used to think that obstacles to love
        Were out of date, the darkened stairs
Leading deprived ones to the mossy tomb
Where she lay carpeted with golden hairs :
        We had no place in such a room,
Belonging to the common ground above.

In sunlight we are free to move, and hold
        Our open assignations, yet
Each love defines its proper obstacles :
Our frowning Montague and Capulet
        Are air, not individuals
And have no faces for their frowns to fold.

Even in sunlight what does freedom mean?
  Romeo's passion rose to fire
From one thin spark within a brace of days.
We for whom time draws out, visas expire,
  Smoulder without a chance to blaze
Upon the unities of a paper scene.

The violence of a picturesque account
  Gives way to details, none the less
Reaching, each one more narrow than the last,
Down to a separate hygienic place
  Where acting love is in the past,
No golden hairs are there, no bleeding count.

No, if there were bright things to fasten on
  There'd be no likeness to the play.
But under a self-generated glare
Any bad end has possibility,
  The means endurance. I declare
I know how hard upon the ground it shone.

The Corridor

A separate place between the thought and felt
The empty hotel corridor was dark.
But here the keyhole shone, a meaning spark.
What fires were latent in it! So he knelt.

Now, at the corridor's much lighter end,
A pierglass hung upon the wall and showed,
As by an easily deciphered code,
Dark, door, and man, hooped by a single band.

He squinted through the keyhole, and within
Surveyed an act of love that frank as air
He was too ugly for, or could not dare,
Or at a crucial moment thought a sin.

Pleasure was simple thus: he mastered it.
If once he acted as participant
He would be mastered, the inhabitant
Of someone else's world, mere shred to fit.

He moved himself to get a better look
And then it was he noticed in the glass
Two strange eyes in a fascinated face
That watched him like a picture in a book.

The instant drove simplicity away —
The scene was altered, it depended on
His kneeling, when he rose they were clean gone
The couple in the keyhole; this would stay.

For if the watcher of the watcher shown
There in the distant glass, should be watched too,
Who can be master, free of others; who
Can look around and say he is alone?

Moreover, who can know that what he sees
Is not distorted, that he is not seen
Distorted by a pierglass, curved and lean?
Those curious eyes, through him, were linked to these —

These lovers altered in the cornea's bend.
What could he do but leave the keyhole, rise,
Holding those eyes as equal in his eyes,
And go, one hand held out, to meet a friend?

Vox Humana

Being without quality
I appear to you at first
as an unkempt smudge, a blur,
an indefinite haze, mere-
ly pricking the eyes, almost
nothing. Yet you perceive me.

I have been always most close
when you had least resistance,
falling asleep, or in bars;
during the unscheduled hours,
though strangely without substance,
I hang, there and ominous.

Aha, sooner or later
you will have to name me, and,
as you name, I shall focus,
I shall become more precise.
O Master (for you command
in naming me, you prefer)!

I was, for Alexander,
the certain victory; I
was hemlock for Socrates;
and, in the dry night, Brutus
waking before Philippi
stopped me, crying out 'Caesar!'

Or if you call me the blur
that in fact I am, you shall
yourself remain blurred, hanging
like smoke indoors. For you bring,
to what you define now, all
there is, ever, of future.

In Santa Maria Del Popolo

Waiting for when the sun an hour or less
Conveniently oblique makes visible
The painting on one wall of this recess
By Caravaggio, of the Roman School,
I see how shadow in the painting brims
With a real shadow, drowning all shapes out
But a dim horse's haunch and various limbs,
Until the very subject is in doubt.

But evening gives the act, beneath the horse
And one indifferent groom, I see him sprawl,
Foreshortened from the head, with hidden face,
Where he has fallen, Saul becoming Paul.
O wily painter, limiting the scene
From a cacophony of dusty forms
To the one convulsion, what is it you mean
In that wide gesture of the lifting arms?

No Ananias croons a mystery yet,
Casting the pain out under name of sin.
The painter saw what was, an alternate
Candour and secrecy inside the skin.
He painted, elsewhere, that firm insolent
Young whore in Venus' clothes, those pudgy cheats,
Those sharpers; and was strangled, as things went,
For money, by one such picked off the streets.

I turn, hardly enlightened, from the chapel
To the dim interior of the church instead,
In which there kneel already several people,
Mostly old women: each head closeted
In tiny fists holds comfort as it can.
Their poor arms are too tired for more than this
— For the large gesture of solitary man,
Resisting, by embracing, nothingness.

The Annihilation of Nothing

Nothing remained: Nothing, the wanton name
That nightly I rehearsed till led away
To a dark sleep, or sleep that held one dream.

In this a huge contagious absence lay,
More space than space, over the cloud and slime,
Defined but by the encroachments of its sway.

Stripped to indifference at the turns of time,
Whose end I knew, I woke without desire,
And welcomed zero as a paradigm.

But now it breaks — images burst with fire
Into the quiet sphere where I have bided,
Showing the landscape holding yet entire:

The power that I envisaged, that presided
Ultimate in its abstract devastations,
Is merely change, the atoms it divided

Complete, in ignorance, new combinations.
Only an infinite finitude I see
In those peculiar lovely variations.

It is despair that nothing cannot be
Flares in the mind and leaves a smoky mark
Of dread.
           Look upward. Neither firm nor free,

Purposeless matter hovers in the dark.

From the Highest Camp

Nothing in this bright region melts or shifts.
The local names are concepts: the Ravine,
Pemmican Ridge, North Col, Death Camp, they mean
The streetless rise, the dazzling abstract drifts,
To which particular names adhere by chance,
From custom lightly, not from character.
We stand on a white terrace and confer;
This is the last camp of experience.

What is that sudden yelp upon the air?
And whose are these cold droppings? whose malformed
Purposeless tracks about the slope? We know.
The abominable endures, existing where
Nothing else can : it is — unfed, unwarmed —
Born of rejection, of the boundless snow.

Innocence

(to Tony White)

He ran the course and as he ran he grew,
And smelt his fragrance in the field. Already,
Running he knew the most he ever knew,
The egotism of a healthy body.

Ran into manhood, ignorant of the past :
Culture of guilt and guilt's vague heritage,
Self-pity and the soul ; what he possessed
Was rich, potential, like the bud's tipped rage.

The Corps developed, it was plain to see,
Courage, endurance, loyalty and skill
To a morale firm as morality,
Hardening him to an instrument, until

The finitude of virtues that were there
Bodied within the swarthy uniform
A compact innocence, child-like and clear,
No doubt could penetrate, no act could harm.

When he stood near the Russian partisan
Being burned alive, he therefore could behold
The ribs wear gently through the darkening skin
And sicken only at the Northern cold,

Could watch the fat burn with a violet flame
And feel disgusted only at the smell,
And judge that all pain finishes the same
As melting quietly by his boots it fell.

Modes of Pleasure

I jump with terror seeing him,
Dredging the bar with that stiff glare
As fiercely as if each whim there
Were passion, whose passion is a whim:

The Fallen Rake, being fallen from
The heights of twenty to middle age,
And helpless to control his rage,
So mean, so few the chances come.

The very beauty of his prime
Was that the triumphs which recurred
In different rooms without a word
Would all be lost some time in time.

Thus he reduced the wild unknown.
And having used each hour of leisure
To learn by rote the modes of pleasure,
The sensual skills as skills alone,

He knows that nothing, not the most
Cunning or sweet, can hold him, still.
Living by habit of the will,
He cannot contemplate the past,

Cannot discriminate, condemned
To the sharpest passion of them all.
Rigid he sits: brave, terrible,
The will awaits its gradual end.

The Byrnies

The heroes paused upon the plain.
When one of them but swayed, ring mashed on ring:
   Sound of the byrnie's knitted chain,
Vague evocations of the constant Thing.

They viewed beyond a salty hill
Barbaric forest, mesh of branch and root
   — A huge obstruction growing still,
Darkening the land, in quietness absolute.

That dark was fearful — lack of presence —
Unless some man could chance upon or win
   Magical signs to stay the essence
Of the broad light that they adventured in.

Elusive light of light that went
Flashing on water, edging round a mass,
   Inching across fat stems, or spent
Lay thin and shrunk among the bristling grass.

Creeping from sense to craftier sense,
Acquisitive, and loss their only fear,
   These men had fashioned a defence
Against the nicker's snap, and hostile spear.

Byrnie on byrnie! as they turned
They saw light trapped between the man-made joints,
   Central in every link it burned,
Reduced and steadied to a thousand points.

Thus for each blunt-faced ignorant one
The great grey rigid uniform combined
   Safety with virtue of the sun.
Thus concepts linked like chainmail in the mind.

Reminded, by the grinding sound,
Of what they sought, and partly understood,
They paused upon that open ground,
A little group above the foreign wood.

Flying Above California

Spread beneath me it lies — lean upland
sinewed and tawny in the sun, and

valley cool with mustard, or sweet with
loquat. I repeat under my breath

names of places I have not been to :
Crescent City, San Bernardino

— Mediterranean and Northern names.
Such richness can make you drunk. Sometimes

on fogless days by the Pacific,
there is a cold hard light without break

that reveals merely what is — no more
and no less. That limiting candour,

that accuracy of the beaches,
is part of the ultimate richness.

Considering the Snail

The snail pushes through a green
night, for the grass is heavy
with water and meets over
the bright path he makes, where rain
has darkened the earth's dark. He
moves in a wood of desire,

pale antlers barely stirring
as he hunts. I cannot tell
what power is at work, drenched there
with purpose, knowing nothing.
What is a snail's fury? All
I think is that if later

I parted the blades above
the tunnel and saw the thin
trail of broken white across
litter, I would never have
imagined the slow passion
to that deliberate progress.

'Blackie, the Electric Rembrandt'

We watch through the shop-front while
Blackie draws stars — an equal

concentration on his and
the youngster's faces. The hand

is steady and accurate;
but the boy does not see it

for his eyes follow the point
that touches (quick, dark movement!)

a virginal arm beneath
his rolled sleeve: he holds his breath.

. . . Now that it is finished, he
hands a few bills to Blackie

and leaves with a bandage on
his arm, under which gleam ten

stars, hanging in a blue thick
cluster. Now he is starlike.

Adolescence

After the history has been made,
and when Wallace's shaggy head

glares on London from a spike, when
the exiled general is again

gliding into Athens harbour
now as embittered foreigner,

when the lean creatures crawl out of
camps and in silence try to live;

I pass foundations of houses,
walking through the wet spring, my knees

drenched from high grass charged with water,
and am part, still, of the done war.

My Sad Captains

One by one they appear in
the darkness: a few friends, and
a few with historical
names. How late they start to shine!
but before they fade they stand
perfectly embodied, all

the past lapping them like a
cloak of chaos. They were men
who, I thought, lived only to
renew the wasteful force they
spent with each hot convulsion.
They remind me, distant now.

34

True, they are not at rest yet,
but now that they are indeed
apart, winnowed from failures,
they withdraw to an orbit
and turn with disinterested
hard energy, like the stars.

Canning Town

No music in this boozer.
She says she's with her
mother, though my
theory is it's a fellow.

I doze into a twilight,
a dry foul taste in my mouth,
nodding on the brown cracked
American leather of the sofa.

The Left-handed Irishman

He raises the pick, point against
the sky, his own weight divided
fairly between his legs,
right hand lower to guide and
steady the handle, left hand
higher to bear the pick down
on the inanimate rubble
which must be broken, levelled
by unskilled labour — But there is
skill in getting the proper
stance — Through an arc the point
falls as force, the human
behind it in control
tiring, but tiring slowly

The Conversation of Old Men

He feels a breeze rise from
the Thames, as far off
as Rotherhithe, in
intimate contact with
water, slimy hulls,
dark wood greenish
at waterline — touching
then leaving what it
lightly touches; he
goes on talking, and this is
the life of wind on water.

The Old Woman

Something approaches, about
which she has heard a good deal.
Her deaf ears have caught it, like
a silence in the wainscot
by her head. Her flesh has felt
a chill in her feet, a draught
in her groin. She has watched it
like moonlight on the frayed wood
stealing toward her
floorboard by floorboard. Will it hurt?

Let it come, it is
the terror of full repose,
and so no terror.

The Goddess

When eyeless fish meet her on
her way upward, they gently
turn together in the dark
brooks. But naked and searching
as a wind, she will allow
no hindrance, none, and bursts up

through potholes and narrow flues
seeking an outlet. Unslowed
by fire, rock, water or clay,
she after a time reaches
the soft abundant soil, which
still does not dissipate her

force — for look ! sinewy thyme
reeking in the sunlight ; rats
breeding, breeding, in their nests ;
and the soldier by a park
bench with his greatcoat collar
up, waiting all evening for

a woman, any woman
her dress tight across her ass
as bark in moonlight. Goddess,
Proserpina : it is we,
vulnerable, quivering,
who stay you to abundance.

Touch

You are already
asleep. I lower
myself in next to
you, my skin slightly

numb with the restraint
of habits, the patina of
self, the black frost
of outsideness, so that even
unclothed it is
a resilient chilly
hardness, a superficially
malleable, dead
rubbery texture.

You are a mound
of bedclothes, where the cat
in sleep braces
its paws against your
calf through the blankets,
and kneads each paw in turn.

Meanwhile and slowly
I feel a is it
my own warmth surfacing or
the ferment of your whole
body that in darkness beneath
the cover is stealing
bit by bit to break
down that chill.

                You turn and
hold me tightly, do
you know who
I am or am I
your mother or
the nearest human being to
hold on to in a
dreamed pogrom.

What I, now loosened,
sink into is an old
big place, it is
there already, for

you are already
there, and the cat
got there before you, yet
it is hard to locate.
What is more, the place is
not found but seeps
from our touch in
continuous creation, dark
enclosing cocoon round
ourselves alone, dark
wide realm where we
walk with everyone.

The Vigil of Corpus Christi

Swaddled to his nose against the chill
he stood all night, like a sentinel
at limits, by the pitted stone wall.

His body was scattered; each grease clot,
each lump and fold in the stiff blanket,
the aches, the circle of his wide hat

touched him at unrelated edges.
But perched above the blanket, his eyes
persisted, trying to become as

steadfast as the dark confronting them.
Then the sky paled: night relinquished him,
like seas casting him up whole through foam.

A footbath clattered in the distance;
his dog ran up and licked him. Each sense
tested itself, sharp from abeyance.

Was this, then, the end of any quest?
the invasion of himself at last
merely by himself? 'To be steadfast,'

he breathed: like a soldier, he straightened.
But the moist tongue went on working round
his ankles; and then, slowly, he grinned

with an unsoldierly joy, at this
soft sweet power awake in his own mass
balanced on his two feet, this fulness.

A Geography

(from *Misanthropos*)

Green overtaking green, it's
endless: squat grasses creep up,
briars cross, heavily weighed
branches overhang, thickets
crowd in on the brown earth gap
in green which is the path made

by his repeated tread, which,
enacting the wish to move,
is defined by avoidance
of loose ground, of rock and ditch,
of thorn-brimmed hollows, and of
poisoned beds. The ground hardens.

Bare within limits. The trick
is to stay free within them.
The path branches, branches still,
returning to itself, like
a discovering system,
or process made visible.

It rains. He climbs up the hill.
Drops are isolate on leaves,
big and clear. It is cool, and
he breathes the barbarous smell
of the wet earth. Nothing moves
at the edges of the mind.

Memoirs of the World

(from *Misanthropos*)

A serving man. Curled my hair,
wore gloves in my cap. I served
all degrees and both sexes.
But I gave readily from
the largess of high spirits,
a sturdy body and strong

fingers. Nor was I servile.
No passer-by could resist
the fragrant impulse nodding
upon my smile. I laboured
to become a god of charm,
an untirable giver.

Needing me, needing me, 'Quick!'
they would call: I came gladly.
Even as I served them sweets
I served myself a trencher
of human flesh in some dark
sour pantry, and munched from it.

My diet, now, is berries,
water, and the gristle of
rodents. I brought myself here,
widening the solitude
till it was absolute. But
at times I am ravenous.

41

A Snow Vision

(from *Misanthropos*)

All that snow pains my eyes, but I stare
on, stare on, lying in my shelter,

feverish, out at the emptiness.
A negative of matter, it is

a dead white surface at random crossed
by thin twigs and bird-tracks on the crust

like fragments of black netting: hard, cold,
wind-swept. But now my mind loses hold

and, servant to an unhinged body,
becoming of it, sinks rapidly

beneath the stitched furs I'm swaddled in,
beneath the stink of my trembling skin,

till it enters the heart of fever,
as its captive, unable to stir.

I watch the cells swimming in concert
like nebulae, calm, without effort,

great clear globes, pink and white. — But look at
the intruder with blurred outline that

glides in among the shoals, colourless,
with tendrils like an anemone's

drifting all around it like long fur,
gently, unintelligently. Where

it touches it holds, in an act of
enfolding, possessing, merging love.

There is coupling where no such should be.
Surely it is a devil, surely

it is life's parody I see, which
enthralls a universe with its rich

heavy passion, leaving behind it
gorgeous mutations only, then night.

It ends. I open my eyes to snow.
I can sleep now; as I drowse I know

I must keep to the world's bare surface,
I must perceive, and perceive what is:

for though the hold of perception must
harden but diminish, like the frost,

yet still there may be something retained
against the inevitable end.

Epitaph for Anton Schmidt

(from *Misanthropos*)

The Schmidts obeyed, and marched on Poland.
And there an Anton Schmidt, Feldwebel,
Performed uncommon things, not safe,
Nor glamorous, nor profitable.

Was the expression on his face
'Reposeful and humane good nature'?
Or did he look like any Schmidt,
Of slow and undisclosing feature?

I know he had unusual eyes,
Whose power no orders might determine,
Not to mistake the men he saw,
As others did, for gods or vermin.

For five months, till his execution,
Aware that action has its dangers,
He helped the Jews to get away
— Another race at that, and strangers.

He never did mistake for bondage
The military job, the chances,
The limits; he did not submit
To the blackmail of his circumstances.

I see him in the Polish snow,
His muddy wrappings small protection,
Breathing the cold air of his freedom
And treading a distinct direction.

Elegy on the Dust

(from *Misanthropos*)

The upper slopes are busy with the cricket;
   But downhill, hidden in the thicket,
Birds alternate with sudden piercing calls
   The rustling from small animals
Retreating, venturing, as they hunt and breed
   Interdependent in that shade.

Beneath it, glare and silence cow the brain
   Where, troughed between the hill and plain,
The expanse of dust waits: acres calm and deep,
   Swathes folded on themselves in sleep
Or waves that, as if frozen in mid-roll,
   Hang in ridged rows. They cannot fall,

44

Yet imperceptibly they shift, at flood,
    In quiet encroachment on the wood —
First touching stalk and leaf with silvery cast,
    They block the pores to death at last
And drift in silky banks around the trunk,
    Where dock and fern are fathoms sunk.

Yet farther from the hill the bowl of dust
    Is open to the casual gust
That dives upon its silence, teasing it
    Into a spasm of wild grit.
Here it lies unprotected from the plain,
    And vexed with constant loss and gain,
It seems, of the world's refuse and debris,
    Turns to a vaguely heaving sea,
Where its own eddies, spouts, and calms appear.
    But seas contain a graveyard : here
The graveyard is the sea, material things
    — From stone to claw, scale, pelt and wings —
Are all reduced to one form and one size.
    And here the human race, too, lies,
An imperfection endlessly refined
    By the imperfection of the mind.
They have all come who sought distinction hard
    To this universal knacker's yard,
Blood dried, flesh shrivelled, and bone decimated :
    Motion of life is thus repeated,
A process ultimately without pain
    As they are broken down again.
The remnants of their guilt mix as they must
    And average out in grains of dust
Too light to act, too small to harm, too fine
    To simper or betray or whine.

Each colourless hard grain is now distinct,
    In no way to its neighbour linked,
Yet from wind's unpremeditated labours
    It drifts in concord with its neighbours,

Perfect community in its behaviour.
   It yields to what it sought, a saviour :
Scattered and gathered, irregularly blown,
   Now sheltered by a ridge or stone,
Now lifted on strong upper winds, and hurled
   In endless hurry round the world.

Pierce Street

Nobody home. Long threads of sunlight slant
Past curtains, blind, and slat, through the warm room.
The beams are dazzling, but, random and scant,
Pierce where they end
                small areas of the gloom
On curve of chairleg or a green stalk's bend.

I start exploring. Beds and canvases
Are shapes in each room off the corridor,
Their colours muted, square thick presences
Rising between
              the ceiling and the floor,
A furniture inferred much more than seen.

Here in the seventh room my search is done.
A bluefly circles, irregular and faint.
And round the wall above me friezes run :
Fixed figures drawn
              in charcoal or in paint.
Out of night now the flesh-tint starts to dawn.

Some stand there as if muffled from the cold,
Some naked in it, the wind around a roof.
But armed, their holsters as if tipped with gold.
And twice life-size —
              in line, in groups, aloof,
They all stare down with large abstracted eyes.

A silent garrison, and always there,
They are the soldiers of the imagination
Produced by it to guard it everywhere.
Bodied within

        the limits of their station
As, also, I am bodied in my skin,

They vigilantly preserve as they prevent
And are the thing they guard, having some time stood
Where the painter reached to make them permanent.
The floorboards creak.

          The house smells of its wood.
Those who are transitory can move and speak.